# It's Easy To Play Schubert.

**Wise Publications**
London/New York/Sydney

Exclusive distributors:
**Music Sales Limited**
8/9 Frith Street, London W1V 5TZ, England.
**Music Sales Limited**
120 Rothschild Avenue, Rosebery, NSW 2018, Australia.

This book © Copyright 1988 by
Wise Publications
UK ISBN 0.7119.1524.5
Order No. AM 71762

Art direction by Mike Bell
Cover illustration by Paul Leith
Compiled by Peter Evans
Arranged by Daniel Scott

Music Sales complete catalogue lists thousands of
titles and is free from your local music book shop,
or direct from Music Sales Limited.
Please send a Cheque or Postal Order for £1.50 for postage to
Music Sales Limited, 8/9 Frith Street, London, W1V 5TZ.

Allegretto from Piano Sonata Op.164, 4
Ave Maria, 6
Ballet Music from Rosamunde, 10
Death And The Maiden, 9
Die Schöne Mullerin Op.25, 14
Entr'acte from Rosamunde, 25
Impromptu Op.90 No.1, 16
Impromptu Op.142, 20
Impromptu Op.142 No.3, 28
Marche Militaire, 18
Moment Musical Op.94 No.3, 30
Piano Trio In E Flat (Slow Movement), 22
Serenade, 32
String Quintet In C (1st Movement), 34
Symphony In B Flat (2nd Movement), 36
Symphony No.9 (Slow Movement), 44
The Trout, 42
Unfinished Symphony (Theme), 38
Wanderer Fantasia, 39
Who Is Sylvia?, 46

# Allegretto from Piano Sonata Op. 164

Composed by Franz Schubert

# Ave Maria

Composed by Franz Schubert

poco rit. . . . . . . . . . . . . . . . . . . . . . . . . . . . . .

a tempo          rit. . . . . . . . . . . . . . . . . . . . . . . . . . . . . . . . . . . . . . . . . . . . . . . . . . . . . . . . . . . . . . . . . .

. . . . . . . . . . . . . . . . . . . . . . . . . . . . a tempo

# Death And The Maiden

Composed by Franz Schubert

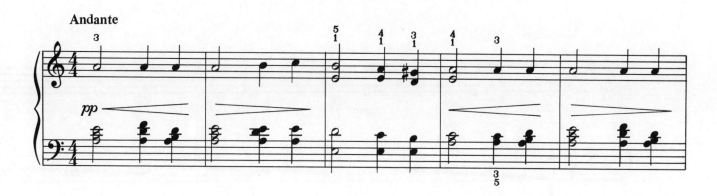

# Ballet Music from Rosamunde

Composed by Franz Schubert

11

poco rit. - - - - - - - - - - - - -

a tempo

# Die Schöne Mullerin Op. 25

Composed by Franz Schubert

# Impromptu Op. 90 No.1

Composed by Franz Schubert

17

# Marche Militaire

Composed by Franz Schubert

# Impromptu Op. 142

Composed by Franz Schubert

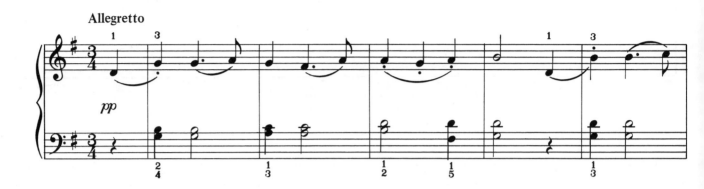

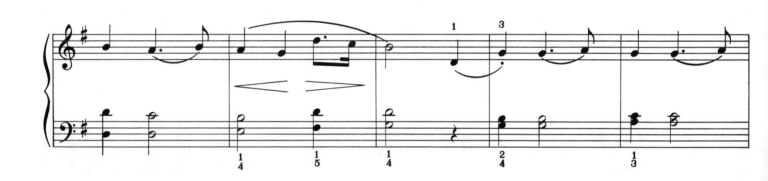

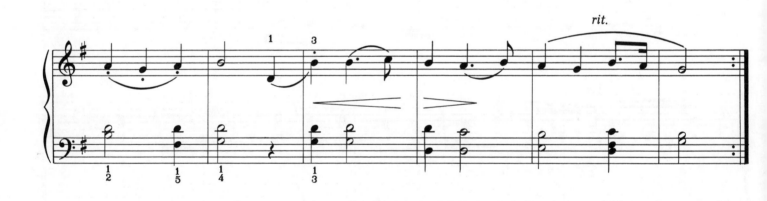

21

# Piano Trio In E Flat
# (Slow Movement)

Composed by Franz Schubert

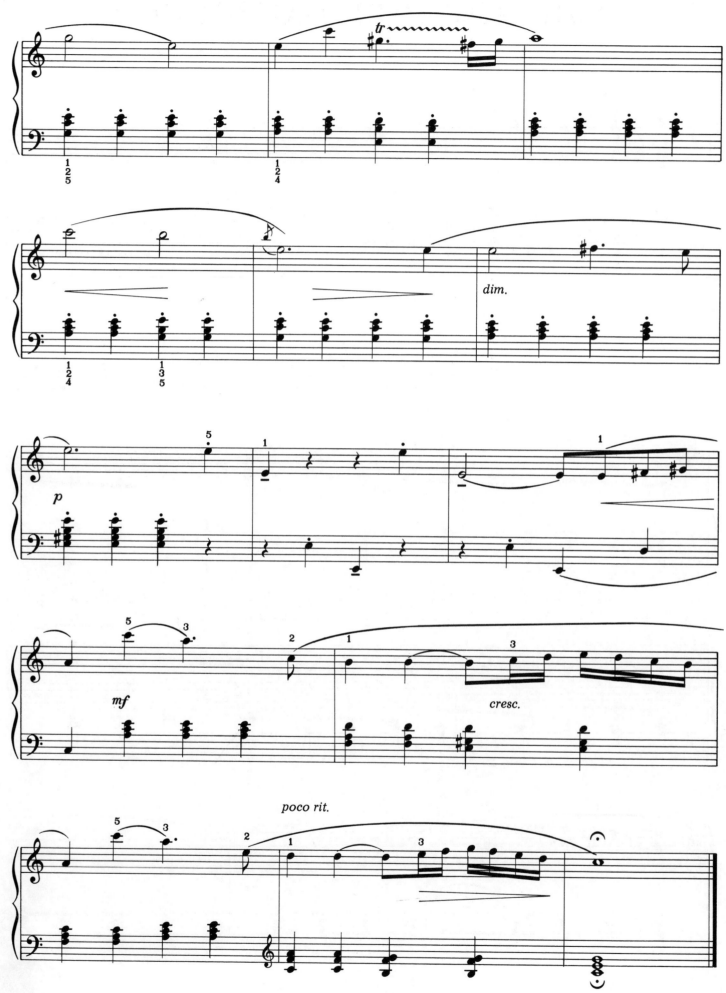

# Entr'acte from Rosamunde

Composed by Franz Schubert

D.C. al Fine

# Impromptu Op. 142 No.3

Composed by Franz Schubert

# Moment Musical Op. 94 No.3

Composed by Franz Schubert

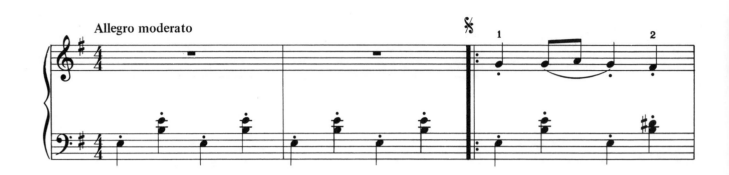

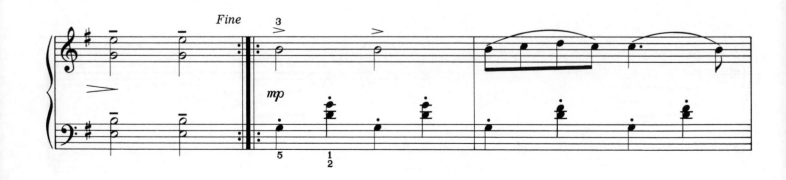

# Serenade

Composed by Franz Schubert

# String Quintet In C
# (1st Movement)

Composed by Franz Schubert

# Symphony In B Flat
# (2nd Movement)

Composed by Franz Schubert

# Unfinished Symphony
## (Theme)

Composed by Franz Schubert

**Allegro moderato**

# Wanderer Fantasia

Composed by Franz Schubert

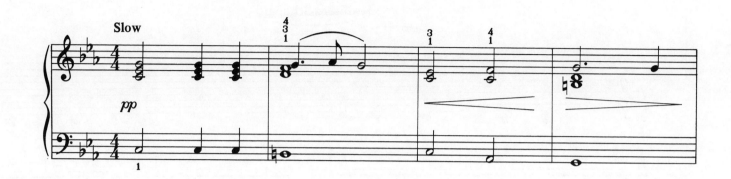

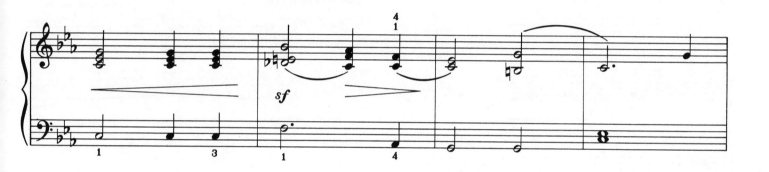

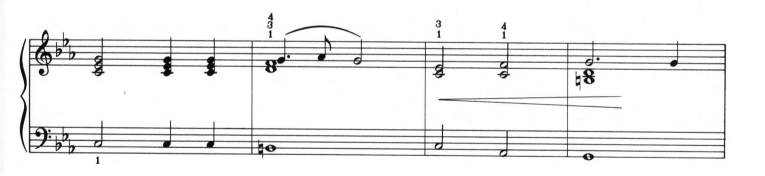

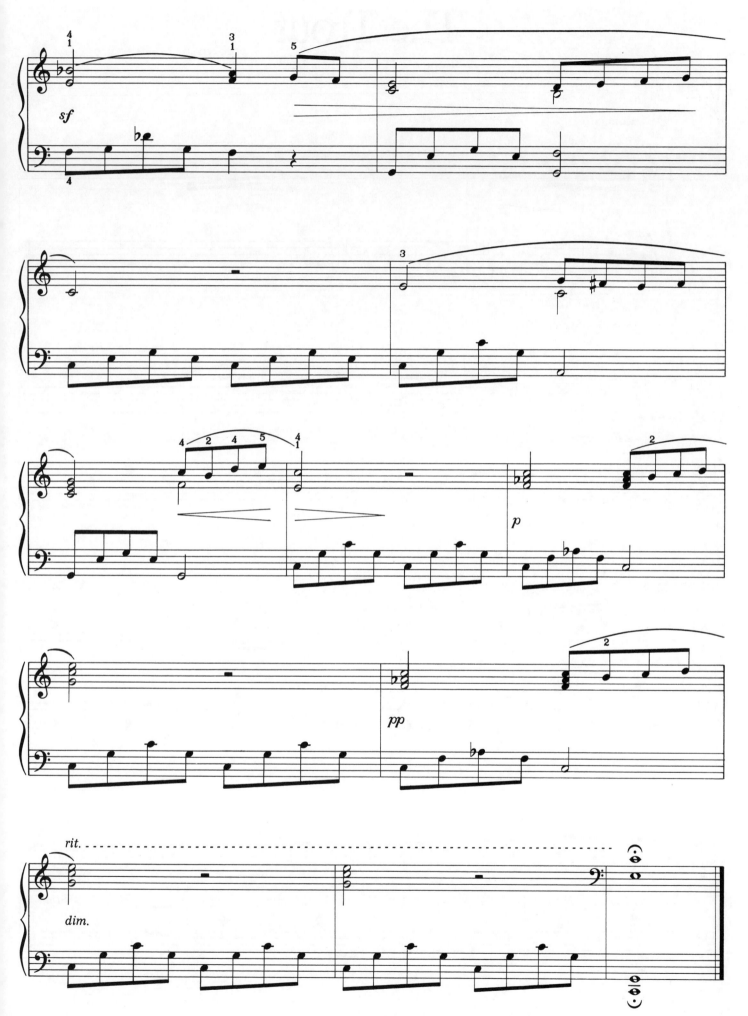

# The Trout

Composed by Franz Schubert

# Symphony No.9
# (Slow Movement)

Composed by Franz Schubert

# Who Is Sylvia?

Composed by Franz Schubert

9/00 (38077)